PRAY and PROSPER

BY

ERNEST HOLMES

Martino Publishing
Mansfield Centre, CT
2011

Martino Publishing
P.O. Box 373,
Mansfield Centre, CT 06250 USA

www.martinopublishing.com

ISBN   978-1-61427-136-9

Cover design by T. Matarazzo

Printed in the United States of America On 100% Acid-Free Paper

PRAY and PROSPER

BY

ERNEST HOLMES

Published by

INSTITUTE OF RELIGIOUS SCIENCE

LOS ANGELES, CALIFORNIA

PRAY AND PROSPER

PRAY and PROSPER

WHAT is prayer? We pray either to an Infinite Mind or an Omnipotent Power. Prayer is always some form of communion with the Universal.

It reaches its highest possibility when it rises above the limitations of any existing circumstance. This is why Jesus told his followers not to judge by appearances. Jesus did not deny the appearance, he merely said do not accept it as the only criterion. How could anyone arrive at such a faith unless he knew that he was dealing with a Power which can rearrange facts and create new ones?

A belief in the Invisible is the very essence of faith. Prayer, or spiritual communion, demands a complete surrender to the Invisible. It knows that because the Creative Power of God is at hand, all things are possible. Man is powerful because he deals with Power. He may become wise because he is immersed in Wisdom. Thus he has an inexhaustable Source from which to draw.

Whatever our idea of God may be, the perception of Reality is always an inner perception. As Moses tells us, the word is not afar off but in our own mouths, and Jesus, that the Kingdom of Heaven is within. The prayer of power is not so much a petition as it is an inner recognition.

We cannot doubt that the Spirit has already made the gift of Life—since we live. Ours is the privilege of acceptance. Thus we are to assume the attitude of a greatful beneficiary of the Divine gifts. This should be done simply and directly. The Spirit is not something that **was,** or that is **going** to be or become. The Truth is that which **is;** it exists at the very center of our being. To pray **in spirit and in truth** means to recognize this indwelling Spirit and to declare the truth about Its activity through us.

God is not poor, weak, sick or unhappy. God is not impoverished, limited or in bondage. It is this Spirit to which we pray, the Reality which we approach at the center of our own being. It is the Silent Partner in every man's life—a wise and loving Presence every ready to respond to us. Since we neither created this Presence nor incarnated It within us, there is nothing we can do but accept It. Jesus said, "Ye must be born again." The second birth is a birth from anpearances to Reality. Robert Browning said. "There is an inmost center in all of us where Truth abides in fullness."

The purpose of prayer, or spiritual communion, is to seek conscious union with this indwelling Presence. Jesus claimed that the words he spoke were not his but were the activity of the Spirit within him. Since there is but One Mind this must be true. It is impossible to lose this "imprisoned splendor" unless we comply with Its nature, which must be Truth, Harmony, and Wholeness.

Hate, disunion, fear and uncertainty may knock at the door of Reality; **only peace can enter.** This is the peace to which Jesus referred when he said, ". . . not as the world giveth, give I unto you. Let not your heart be troubled, neither let it be afraid." Peace is at the very center of our being. Sometimes we arrive merely at a partial unity with Spirit. At other times we more completely enter into the contemplation of Reality. Always our prayer will be as effective as is the realization generated in the act of communion. Thus our words become "clothed upon" with the living Presence of an invisible Power ever projecting Itself into form through our meditation.

There is a Law of Mind which follows the pattern of our thought. This Law works automatically. It is a mechanical law and a mathematical one. It is the Law of Cause and Effect. We should not have any anxious thought concerning the operation of this Law; It will always respond by corresponding. Thus Jesus said that it is done unto us **as** we believe. The word **as** is important since it implies that the Creative Intelligence, in working **for** us, must work **through** us at the level of our acknowledgment of It as working. This is praying **in spirit and in truth,** and according to law. And there must be law even in prayer, if there is to be Cosmic order.

Spiritual communion is deeper than intellectual perception. The prayer of the intellect may be perfect in form; but this form must be warmed and colored by feeling and conviction. The Bible refers both to the "letter" and the "spirit" of the Law. It implies that both are necessary. That is, we should not only state our word definitely, but we must believe it sincerely, deeply. Paul tells us to be transformed by the renewing of the mind. We must cast off the intellectual doubt which affirms that things must continue as they always have been. We must enter into a deep, spiritual communion with Reality, realizing that a new creation is taking place through our consciousness. This judgment may be contrary to appearances, but it is nevertheless a true judgment.

Man's mind has been likened to the "Workshop of God" for it is here that the tools of thought consciously may fashion destiny, may carve out a new future. We have been told to do this according to the pattern shown us in the Mount. This means that we are to formulate our ideas on the proposition that there is an all-sustaining Power and an all-pervading Presence around us, and an immutable Law ever serving us when our lives are in harmony with the Divine Nature. Through an exact law, demonstration follows the word of faith. This law is a law of polarity, of reflection, of cause and effect. It is written that "I will be to them as they have spoken." Again, "Be firm and ye shall be made firm." "Act as though I am, and I will be." This calls for a surrender of the intellect to a spiritual conviction which dares to believe, disregarding any evidence to the contrary.

We must continue in faith until our whole mental life, both conscious and subjective, responds. If we would pray and prosper we must believe that the Spirit is both willing and able to make the gift. But since the Spirit can only give us what we take, and since the taking is a mental act, we must train the mind to believe and accept. This is the secret of the power of prayer.

One need not have great intellectual attainmant to understand these simple things. Jesus said that the Kingdom of Heaven is reached through childlike faith. Again he said, "I thank thee, Father . . . because thou hast hid these things from the wise and the prudent, and hast revealed them unto babes." Everything that Jesus said and did was said and done to provide an example for our benefit. His whole life and teaching was to describe the nature of Reality. All of his works, which have been miscalled miracles, were to prove that his teaching was correct. He asked those around him whether it was easier to announce a philosophy or to prove it. They had been arguing about his spiritual authority and

11

he asked them ". . . whether it is easier to say, Thy sins be forgiven thee; or to say, Arise and walk." And that they might know that "the Son of man hath power on earth to forgive sins," he said to the man with palsy, "Arise, take up thy bed, and go unto thine house."

Just as the teachings of Jesus announce the Divine Presence, so his works prove the presence of a Law which received the impress of his word and brought it forth into form. He asked no authority other than that which was demonstrated through his act. Since Jesus taught the most definite system of spiritual thought ever given to the world, as well as the most simple and direct, and since he was able to prove his teaching by his works, we could do no better than to follow his example. There are two ways in which we may do this. One is blind faith, and we cannot doubt its effectiveness; the other is through coming to understand what the teachings of Jesus really meant. Thus knowledge passes into a faith so complete that it is unshakable.

Jesus gave specific instructions for prayer. He likened the Divine Spirit to a Heavenly Father, and he placed the Kingdom of this Spirit at the center of Man's being.

Our Father which art in heaven. The God Principle within us; the eternal Truth within us; the everlasting Presence within us.

Hallowed be thy name. Thy name is perfect;

12

It is the all-inclusive name of the "I am" beside which there is none other. It is the One, Only and All which includes everything that was, is, or is to be. The same yesterday, today and forever.

Thy kingdom come. Thy will be done in earth, as it is in heaven. When the Kingdom of God is perceived and the Will and Nature of God understood, then shall the Power within us recreate and control our environment after the pattern of Wholeness and Abundance. When that which is without shall be controlled by that which is within; when the Kingdom of God comes on earth among men, It will heal all nations of sickness, war and poverty, for the Kingdom of God is Wholeness, Unity and Peace.

Give us this day our daily bread. This is an acknowledgment that Substance forever takes form in our affairs as "manna from heaven." "Give us this day our daily bread." This is meant to include everything we shall ever need, whether it be a house to live in, an automobile to ride in (in our day), a suit of clothes to wear, bread to eat and butter to put on the bread. It includes, according to the words of Jesus, "what things soever ye desire." We must, however, be certain that the desire is consistent with the nature of Reality; and we may be certain that if our desire is toward a greater degree of livingness for ourselves and others, and harms no one, then it is

13

the Divine Will. "Give us this day our daily bread," includes everything we can ever need—friendship, love, beauty, peace, poise and power—for God in not only All, He is All-in-all and through all.

And forgive us our debts, as we forgive our debtors. We might say with Shakespeare, "There's the rub," for it is a bold statement that mere protestations do not suffice. We must actually partake of the Divine Nature if we are to portray It. We must forgive if we are to be forgiven, we must love if we would be loved. "Give, and it shall be given unto you; good measure, pressed down, and shaken together, and running over, shall men give into your bosom." And we must not overlook another statement of Jesus, "Judge not, that ye be not judged. For with what judgment ye judge, ye shall be judged; and with what measure ye mete, it shall be measured to you again." Once more, there's the rub: do we forsake all animosity in our desire to surrender our entire being to love? Jesus plainly tells us that it is useless to lay our gifts upon the altar while our own mind is diseased with animosity and with strife. "Forgive us our debts, as we forgive our debtors." This is the Law of Cause and Effect. There is no escape from it.

And lead us not into temptation, but deliver us from evil. The All-Creative Truth can never lead us into temptation, but an acknowledgment

14

of Its presence and a desire to embody Its essence delivers us from every form of evil. "He shall give his angels charge over thee to keep thee in all thy ways."

For thine is the kingdom, and the power, and the glory, for ever. The Kingdom, the Power and the Glory of Reality never change. They are always the same, ever available, unwavering, consistent. The glory of Truth, the kingdom of Reality and the power of Law are ever with us. It is also written that "as many as received him, to them gave he the power." That is, to those who embody and acknowledge the nature of Reality, is given the power to portray It. Not only to drink from the well-springs of life but to pass the refreshing draught to others. Jesus very definitely taught that when we have complied with the Divine Nature, then we shall have a power at our command which will be irresistible. His teaching was so simple and yet so profound; so quiet and yet so dynamic, it will yet revolutionize human conduct.

Jesus left very implicit instructions relative to prayer. It was one of the customs at that time for people to stand at the street corners and pray, using a loud voice, petitioning God with vehemance, screaming their affirmations, proclaiming their denunciations; sometimes in wrath, sometimes in fear, and sometimes with reverence. This rather boisterous and noisy approach to the Spirit

15

did not disturb Jesus. With a calm sense that every man is rewarded according to his own consciousness, disregarding what his particular method may be, Jesus said, "Verily I say unto you, They have their reward." What magnificent understanding! What depth of reason! What profound insight into Reality! Jesus did not condemn, but in teaching his more intimate followers, those to whom he said it was given "to know the mysteries of the kingdom," Jesus counselled another approach, calm, simple, direct, and childlike.

First of all he said, "Judge not according to appearances." That is, do not be confused by the conditions around you. The waves may be turbulent and the boat storm tossed. This appearance is real enough, but do not be confused over it. "Be still, and know that I am God." This is the supreme test. "Judge not according to appearances." They may appear dismal and forlorn, or as hideous monsters rising out of the deep, but I shall command them to be still, "It is I who speak unto you." The inner Spirit is proclaiming Its own nature; It is announcing Its own program.

This is the first great instruction of Jesus—to have such faith and confidence in the Invisible that appearances no longer disturb you. Are there five thousand people waiting to be fed and only a basketful of loaves and fishes, brought by a small boy for his own lunch, as he sat listening in wonder to the words this man spoke as man never spake before? Jesus did not say: Send the multitude home! But with confidence and faith he calmly said, in substance, "Let them be seated; make them comfortable; remove their fear; break down the barriers; let us bless the bread and the fish; and let the Lord of the Harvest increase the supply and feed the famished." Jesus was not afraid when they brought the insane boy to him. Calmly he spoke to his troubled thought and stilled the strife that was raging in the mind of the demented. This, then, is the first great lesson —"Judge not according to appearances."

Next we come to the preparation for prayer. Having shut out all appearances to the contrary, enter the closet. Jesus was not referring to any physical room or hiding place. To enter the closet means to withdraw into one's own thought, to shut out all confusion and discord. Here is the silence of the soul look to the All-Creative Wisdom and Power, to the ever-present Substance. When we have entered the closet and shut the door to outward appearances, we are to make known our requests—"what things soever ye desire."

Next Jesus tells us that we are to **believe that we actually possess** the objects of our desire, disregarding all appearances to the contrary. We are to enter into this invisible inheritance acting as though it were true. Our faith in the substance of the Invisible is to take actual form. The Divine Giver Himself is to make the gift, but first we must believe that we have received it, and then we shall receive it—". . . believe that ye receive them, and ye shall have them." This is a veiled statement of the Law of Cause and Effect operating in human affairs. When we have believed that we have, we have actually given birth to the form that is to be presented. Having made known our request with thanksgiving and received the answer with gratitude, we must rest assured that the Law will bring about the desired result.

"Thy Father which seeth in secret himself shall reward thee openly." Everything passes from the Invisible into the visible to be temporarily experienced and again to be withdrawn. This is the eternal play of Life upon Itself; the eternal act of creation. "Thy Father which seeth in secret himself shall reward thee openly." Rest in peace knowing that it is done. This profound principle which Jesus announced (and the simple technique of its use in which he counselled his followers) exists today in all of its fullness. It is the very cornerstone upon which our philosophy is built.

Suppose we call this prayer a treatment, and its answer a demonstration. Would it not logically follow that, since the law which Jesus announced when he said, "what things soever ye desire," is a law of reflection, each treatment or

18

prayer should be definite? In every case, one would have to convince himself that whatever is specified in his treatment or prayer will be brought about. Thus each one becomes inspired by the Divine Presence and specalizes the Creative Principle for his individual use or for the use of others.

The following examples of the possibility of prayer, merely suggest certain ways in which this may be accomplished.

* * * *

Prayer Is Mind in Action

Prayer is a thing of thought and feeling, therefore, it is Mind in action. God is Infinite Knowingness. We cannot explain creation on any basis other than that this Infinite Knowingness, moving as Law, produces form. The mathematics of this Mind must be exact.

Prayer is a movement through our consciousness upon the universe itself. It is the Law of Mind in action. Whenever our acceptance makes it possible, there will be an answer to our prayer which will mathematically correspond to the use we have been making of this Law of Mind. Jesus tells us that when we comply with the Law it is done unto us as we believe. We cannot doubt that Jesus was teaching the Law of Mind in action; the exercise of the God Power within us as a mathematical sequence of cause and effect.

Since prayer is Mind in action, we must be

19

certain that the thoughts running through our prayers are those of exalted acceptance; of complete fulfillment, here and now.

Prayer Invokes the Mental Law

Even in divine communion we are dealing with the Law of Cause and Effect. Our prayer invokes this Divine Law and causes It to manifest in our external world at the level of our inner perception of Its working. Because this is true, prayer should always be definite, conscious and active.

When we plant a garden we invoke the creative fertility of the soil for definite purposes; we specialize its creative action that it may fulfill specific desires. And in the greater garden of the soul, the garden of the Life Principle Itself, where we deal with thoughts and ideas as seeds, we should follow the same pattern.

We should never forget that all physical nature is merely an out-picturing of the Invisible Cause which gives rise to it. Thus we are told to make known our requests with thanksgiving. But this is also a definite state. Not only should we assume the position of a thankful receiver, we should also assume the intelligent position of one who makes known his concrete requests. "What things soever ye desire" should consciously be accepted. In this way we invoke the Law of Cause and Effect for specific purposes. In this way the Law, which is the servant of the Lord, serves us. This is Its nature. This is the will of the Divine Being.

Prayer as Communion

Communion is not petition; it is an inward sense of Reality; it is something we sense, feel and respond to. We have a good illustration of this in Moses at the burning bush. All nature, as Browning tells us, is alive, awake and aware with the potent Presence.

Communion is entering into conscious union with the essence of things. When we commune with nature she speaks to us, as the poet has suggested, in various ways. The burning bush spoke to Moses and proclaimed the presence of God. He realized he was on holy ground—all nature became animated with the Divine. Everywhere he looked he saw God. This is communion.

We must learn to commune with the indwelling Spirit; to feel Its presence; to sense Its power and to respond to Its influence. This is entirely a thing of feeling.

Spiritual Identification through Communion

We all know that it is impossible for one to become successful unless he first identifies himself with success. The great identification is with the "I Am" in the midst of our being. "The Lord thy God in the midst of thee, is mighty" to heal and to prosper.

If we wish love and friendship we must identify ourselves with them; we must embody them in our thinking. Spirit is the great actor, the final Cause of everything. It is with this inner Spirit that we commune. This is the meaning of prayer; to commune with the Spirit which is already within us; to identify ourselves with It, following which we automatically project this identification into our experience. The effect of the old mistakes is wiped out; old memory images are loosened until their content no longer harms. We are identified with the stream of accomplishment, the certainty that spiritual laws guide and protect us; and no evil can befall this identification. **This act of spiritual identification, through conscious communion, is one of the supreme accomplishments of the soul.**

Shifting the Burden

Bunyan tells us in **Pilgrim's Progress** that burdens drop from our shoulders as we scale the heights. The burden falls back into the **slough of** despond from which we have so recently emerged in our upward climb. Spiritual communion has this effect upon us. As consciousness ascends in realization, burdens gradually loosen themselves and roll backward, disappearing into the oblivion of their native nothingness. Thus prayer shifts the burden by entering into partnership with the Divine.

Prayer ties us to a Power that is able, ready and willing to fulfill every legitimate desire; to bring every good thing to us; to do for us even more abundantly than we have expected. ". . . before they call, I will answer; and while they are yet speaking, I will hear." This shifting of the burden is important for when we feel isolated, alone and struggling against tremendous odds, we are not equal to the task before us. Life becomes a drudgery rather than a **jubilant beholding.** But if we know the burden is lifted and set upon the shoulders of the Law, then power and speed come to hands and feet; joy floods the imagination with anticipation. We must learn to shift the burden to the perfect Law.

The Secret Place of the Most High

Where is the Secret Place of the Most High other than in our own consciousness? It is written that "he that dwelleth in the secret place of the most High shall abide under the shadow of the Almighty." The word "shadow" is used because it suggests protection: the refreshing coolness of the shadow of a rock in a desert place. The shadow of the Almighty means a place of protection, a place of peace. **But before we reach this place of protection we must dwell in the Secret Place of the Most High.** Since Spirit is everywhere present, It must be where we are. Therefore the Secret Place of the Most High is not a place at all but a state of consciousness, a contemplation of Reality.

The Secret Place of the Most High is at the center of our own being, where in silence we wait on Spirit and permit the Perfect Law to fulfill our desire. This is waiting upon the Lord. We permit the Divine images of perfection to flow through our consciousness, reflecting themselves through the Law of Cause and Effect into our objective conditions.

There is no confusion in this Secret Place; none can enter It for us; none can prohibit Its entrance to us. The door is always open, the gate ever ajar. The Secret Place of the Most High is a place of light, of illumination, of poise and assurance. It is a place of rest.

Prayer as a Transforming Power

Silent contemplation of the Divine Presence transmutes lower energies into higher ones. This transmutation of the lower into the higher, a quest of the alchemists of old, is now recognized in the science of psychology. It is called "sublimation" which means transforming chaotic energies of the psyche into constructive outlets of self-expression. If this can be done on a psychological basis, how much more certain it is that the transforming power of spiritual vision will transmute every negation into a positive affirmation.

Prayer can convert disease into health, poverty

into wealth, misery into happiness. It can transmute our beliefs in the devil, or evil, into a picture of an Angel of Light, a guardian angel ever protecting us, forever going before and preparing the way; forever making perfect, plain and immediate the way; forever announcing, "I am the way, the truth and the life." This transforming power of silent communion is manifest as our spiritual vision looks up and not down.

The Word of Power

"He taught them as one having authority, and not as the scribes." In silent communion with the Infinite, we create a consciousness of power through the recognition of the Divine Presence. Jesus said all Power is delivered unto the Son. Prayer is a conscious acceptance of this Power; a joyful recognition of the Divine Presence; a grateful acknowledgment of protection and guidance, of wholeness and of peace. All Power is given unto the Son. Prayer enables us to contact this Power and to make definite use of It for beneficent purposes, to heal to prosper, to make happy, to reveal the wholeness in everything.

Every man has this Power. Plotinus spoke of it as a power which all men possess, but which few use. The bible tells us to stir up the gift that is within us. We must enter into the consciousness of power. This is done through silent recognition, acknowledgment, acceptance and definite projection. Prayer not only receives the Divine Power, it projects it into manifestation. Prayer directs the Invisible Power for definite purposes. It does this by acknowledging the Power and by accepting that It has no opposites. Nothing hinders Spirit; nothing limits the Infinite; there are no obstructions to It. We are told that this Power breaks down the iron doors, and the gates of brass. It penetrates every apparently solid object; It dissolves every obstruction; It creates every desired form. Such is the dynamic power of this silent communion with Reality.

Prayer Reflects

The reflection of an image in a mirror is an exact likeness of the image which is held before the mirror. So the Law of Cause and Effect reflects back to us a likeness of the images of our thought. Thus we are told that we reflect the glory of God. But too often we reflect the fear and limitation of man rather than the glory of God.

We must find new meanings to life if we hope to create new images which, in their turn, will supply new reflections. Jesus told us to judge not according to appearances but to judge righteously. If we judge only according to what is now transpiring, our reflection of these images will merely perpetuate the old limitation, but if we judge righteously, that is, if we look into the omnipotence of Good, we shall create new images of thought which will reflect greater abundance.

Prayer, then, is a mirror reflecting the images of our thought through the Law of good into our outward experiences. What are we reflecting, the glory of God or the confusion of man?

Concentration and Visualization in Prayer

Prayer does not concentrate Substance, it merely focalizes our attention upon It. The Spirit is already omnipresent. We do not gather the principle of mathematics together and pile it up or concentrate it for our use; we merely draw upon it. So it is in the act of prayer. **It is attention and not concentration; willingness and not will.**

The very idea that we must concentrate something suggests coercion. It suggests a reluctance on the part of the Law or the Spirit in its response to us. It suggests laborious effort. The Spirit never exerts effort, It merely remolds Itself in the form of Its own desire, and immediately experiences the form, because It reflects Its own glory in the law of Its own Being. There is nothing to concentrate, nothing to force, nothing to argue with, nothing to oppose.

If we wish to demonstrate that prayer or spiritual communion is a potent force, we must believe that both Energy and Divine Action are at our disposal; that the Creative Genius of the universe is already wherever we focus our attention. We must **permit** rather than petition.

Prayer Removes Tension

Spiritual communion is relaxing. There is neither stress nor strain in it. All the yesterdays of fear and failure are dropped from consciousness; today everything is filled with peace and joy. Jesus said, "My yoke is easy, and my burden is light." The Spirit has no burden, creates none and enters into none. As Emerson said, "It is the finite alone that has wrought and suffered, the Infinite lies stretched in smiling repose."

Spiritual communion is letting go of all negation; a reaching out and up toward freedom, wholeness and happiness. It is a calm, inward sense of Reality. There is no struggle, no tension, only peace. Since we are dealing with a power which can easily accomplish our desired good and give to us more abundantly even than we are able to receive, there should be no sense of compulsion, but rather a relaxed, yet an attentive and active, acceptance. All anxiety is dropped by the wayside.

Over-anxiety is one of the most negative states of mind we can experience. It is a complete denial of the Divine Beneficence, a feeling that the entire burden of life rests upon our shoulders. Spiritual communion relieves this tension, auto-

28

matically straightens out the consciousness. Through recognition, acknowledgment and receptivity it readjusts the psychic stream of life. It frees the pent-up emotions and causes them to become sublimated or transformed into the energy of light, of power and of self-expression. Jesus tells us to take no anxious thought for the morrow. All of our tomorrows are still unborn; every day should view a new creation, a world more blessed than yesterday.

Anxiousness and anxiety arise from a sense of uncertainty of the future, not from frustrations of the past. We are to take no anxious thought for tomorrow. This does not mean that we are to act in an irresponsible or chaotic manner. It merely means that we are to live this day in calm confidence of the future. All of our memories of the past will be healed and all the pent-up energies of unexpressed desires will flow out from us in joyful expression, if our communion with nature and with the Spirit becomes complete. This is why quiet and secluded spots tend to rest us. But the only quiet and secluded spot in all the universe is at the center of our own being where pure Spirit reigns supreme.

Prayer Converts Substance into Action and Supply

If we would pray and prosper we should realize that we are surrounded by a spiritual Substance which is forever taking the form of supply. Wherever we look we should see right action. Spiritual communion enables us to do this. It lifts our thought above the solid fact of a situation or circumstance. It resolves the fact into a fluid and remolds it into a new form; straightens out the lines of our energy, into harmonious currents of self-expression.

There is but one final Essence, which is pure Spirit. The act of prayer in spiritual communion lifts the conciousness into a perception of this Essence flowing out into action. At the center of everything there is Something which never moves, and yet all movement takes place within It. There is Something which Itself is not caused but from which all effect flows. Therefore Essence is both cause and effect. It is the actor, act and action.

Everything moves in circles, and when we silently contemplate the invisible Essence moving in our affairs, we shall discover that our thought comes back to us laden with the fruits of our expectation.

Some of the ancients spoke of the Karmic Law, or what today we call the Law of Cause and Effect, as the result of the fruits of our action. If we would have these fruits abundant, we must think of the Essence as forever passing into form; forever flowing around us, pressing against us, flowing out into everything we do; flowing into health, happiness and prosperity.

Prayer in Action

Evelyn Underhill tells us that our lives should swing between prayer, meditation and action. We used to pray, "Now I lay me down to sleep, I pray the Lord my soul to keep; if I should die before I wake, I pray the Lord my soul to take." Someone has suggested that we add to this beautiful evening prayer one for the new day: "Now I get me up to work, I pray the Lord I shall not shirk; if I should die before the night, I pray the Lord my work's done right."

It is not intended that we should spend all of our time in inaction, for the very law of our being is Mind acting. An active thought will always find itself surrounded with intelligant, objective activities. The passing of human events is no mere illusion, it is a logical and legitimate activity of Mind finding fulfillment. It is the action of a "jubiliant and beholding soul" proclaiming God's works to be good. Every act should become a prayer, as Brother Lawrence so beautifully expressed in his life, which was the conscious practicing of the Divine Presence.

If God is in all events, then we should go forth gladly to meet them. Not only in the stillness of the evening, or the quiet of midnight, but also in the rising tide of human endeavor when the spiritual sun climbs high, flooding the earth with its effulgent glory, is the presence of God revealed.

Joy and Enthusiasm

It has been said that joy infuses the commonplace with a creative activity. Emerson said the only thing he learned about grief was its emptiness. Jesus spoke of the joy which he had and which he desired his disciples to have, that their joy might be full. There is a song at the center of everything. The music of the spheres is no illusion. We must uncover the song and permit it to saturate our souls with joy.

Enthusiasm is the most creative of all the imaginative faculties. There is something light, unobstructed, weightless about it. We cannot associate the Spirit with sadness or depression. The very thought of the "Fountain of Life" suggests something gushing forth, bubbling up from a subterranean passage, whose flow is irresistible. It is no wonder that the ancients said that the wind whispers, the leaves clap their hands and the morning stars sing together. We are told that the shepherds heard this celestial music, the angelic chorus singing "Peace on earth, good will toward men."

Spiritual communion will cause the angels of our better self to sing, making our consciousness happy. Spiritual communion is not a droll affair, it is not a wailing wall, it is the triumphant pro-

cession of the soul into the Secret Place of the
Most High, where the scroll of life is taken from
the Ark of the Covenant, on which are inscribed
the joyous words, "I am the Lord thy God in the
midst of thee."

The Prayer of Thanksgiving

"Enter into his gates with thanksgiving;" "Make
a joyfull noise unto the Lord;" "Bless the Lord, O
my soul: and all that is within me, bless his holy
name."

We are told to make known our requests with
thanksgiving, and why shouldn't we be great-
full when we realize that the Divine gift is forever
made? Why shouldn't our spirits rise in joyful
praise to the Life Principle which has delivered
Its entire nature to us, witholding nothing?

We know that when we praise animals they
respond to us. We know that when we praise chil-
dren they co-operate with us. Since the intelligence operating through animal and child responds
to praise and thanksgiving, why shouldn't everything respond in like manner? There is but one
Spirit in all things.

When we condemn any physical organ, we re-
tard the circulation of the life forces through it.
Therefore, Jesus tells us to judge not that we be
not judged. We should praise every organ of
the body—"Bless the Lord, O my soul; and all
that is within me, bless his holy name." We should

bless the action and the reaction of the life forces that flow through the body. We should bless everything that we do; everyone we meet, every letter we write, every person we think of, every incident that comes into our imagination. The desert is made to bloom and blossom as the rose, by blessing it with the presence of seed, water, personal attention and cultivation. The music of the spheres is heard only by those who listen— not with an ear dulled by condemnation and censure, but with praise and thanksgiving.

The Self-creative Energy of Prayer

Dr. Carrel, in an article on prayer, has suggested that faith is a luminous and self-creative energy. Faith lays hold of a Power which is not only creative, but which creates out of Its own being. It is self-energizing.

The creative energy of Spirit must be limitless. Therefore we can set no limit to the possibility of what it can do for us. Undoubtedly It is able to give us infinitely more than we have expected, understood or accepted. We must believe that It will not only make the gift, It will also, out of Its own energy, out of Its own power, out of Its own Being, create the way, the method and the means through which the gift is to come to us.

This is the Reality with which prayer deals. Infinite in Its possibility, ever ready to respond, the Creative Spirit awaits our recognition. We must learn to have faith, to walk in the light.

34

The Field of Faith

Wherever people meet together for prayer and spiritual communion, a field of faith is created which reacts upon everyone who enters it. An atmosphere of Reality has been recognized; a new vibratory law has been set in motion. It is easy to break one twig, but if we bind many twigs together they become unbreakable. In group consciousness, the individual faith of each member is strengthened through union with all the others. "In union there is strength," is just as true in our mental life as it is in the body of our affairs.

Always we should seek the companionship of those whose faith may be added to ours. Thought atmospheres are real enough. We sense them in the quiet of the cathedral or at shrines where countless thousands have gathered with uplifted faith, seeking communion with the Eternal Reality. Thus the power of one is multiplied through combining it with the power of others. This is not because the Spirit listens to **many** more than to just one, but because often many create a larger hope and a greater expectancy. They develop a real dynamic field of faith.

Prayer and Recognition

The art of prayer arrives at a point of certainty when it recognizes the gift even before it is made. In the creative order everything passes from the invisible into the visible through the act of idea manifesting itself as form. Therefore Jesus told his followers to pray, believing that they had and they would receive.

Recognition is an image of acceptance held in mind until the condition accepted appears either in the body or in the affairs. We are either accepting or rejecting at all times. We are either recognizing the Divine Principle as goodness or as evil. We cannot be too careful in studying to attain recognition. This really means that we must look into what appears to be empty space, into a void, and see a solid rock upon which the feet of faith may be planted. Always the rock appears out of the void through recognition.

The reason for this is plain. Everything Jesus said and did was descriptive of the Divine Nature and of the Law of Cause and Effect. He knew how things work from the invisible to the visible, and when he told us to recognize and accept, he knew what he was talking about. We must learn to recognize the gift even before it is made.

Prayer as Petition

". . . nevertheless not my will, but thine, be done." This petition is not to a far-away God who may or may not respond. It is the recognition of the Divine Presence which is always ready and willing to respond. True prayer always says, "Thy will be done." An intelligent perspective of Truth recognizes that the Will of God and the Nature of the Divine Being are identical. God cannot will anything other than perfection; God cannot will anything other than abundance; God cannot will anything other than goodness, truth and beauty.

Submission to a superior Intelligence, not to an opposing power. Our request is made as to a friend who we know is both able and willing to respond. Therefore, the petition becomes a joyful recognition of the fact that "before they call I will answer." "Father, I thank thee that thou hast heard me. And I knew that thou hearest me always"—these words of Jesus give us an example of petition and acceptance.

It is the recognition of the Spirit as a Friend, and the acceptance that this Friend acts in our behalf immediately, and with power, that brings the answer. Do we not pray for a harvest when we plant the seed? Are not seed time and harvest two ends of one law of cause and effect? Petition and acceptance are two ways of recognizing the Divine Giving which says, "Son, thou art ever with me, and all that I have is thine."

Prayer as a Science

We should not think it strange to speak of prayer as scientific. Science is a knowledge of laws and causes. The principle of any science has always existed. The discovery of such a principle and the gradual accumulation of facts relative to it, prepare the way for a technique for its use.

This is also true of prayer. We know that throughout the ages, at all times and under all situations, prayers have been answered by some invisible Agency which apparently is no respecter of persons, times, races, creeds or cultures, but which forevermore proclaims, "Whosoever will, may come."

The Agency which answers prayer is not concerned over particular religious convictions; never does it ask if we are intellectual, cultured or ignorant; it responds alike to all. It is impersonal. But since some prayers have not been answered, it is self-evident that the Power which answers, must do so only under certain conditions. It is reasonable to assume that the one praying, either consciously or unconsciously has supplied the necessary conditions which make possible the granting of his request; that there is a science of prayer; that prayer deals not only with a Divine Beneficence but also with a law of Cause and Effect.

The Art of Prayer

Prayer is more than an intellectual petetion; it is a thing of feeling; a creative act. Just as an artist feels beauty, rather than sees it, so we feel the Divine Presence as warmth, color and life, ever responding to us. There is an artistry in spiritual communion: a combination of mental attitudes, of states of consciousness, of thoughts, words and feelings, which, combined, produce a subjective pattern of unity, harmony and beauty.

Prayer is both an art and a science. Scientifically, it has form; artistically, it has color, feeling, conviction. Perhaps it is the finest of all arts. The approach to Spirit is entirely a thing of feeling. This feeling rises out of conviction, an intuitional sense, an inner witness. There is something within us which knew Reality long before the conscious intelligence was born. We feel our way back to the original Creative Genius of the universe, the infinite Artist whose creations are spread throughout all time and space.

The Prayer of Acceptance

Jesus plainly taught his followers that prayers would be answered when the one praying **accepted the answer.** This is why it is written that "the prayer of faith shall save the sick, and the Lord shall raise him up." This gives us an interesting side light on the Divine Law. First we have a prayer of faith, one of complete acceptance. We have an affirmation which completely embodies an idea. We believe. This is the prayer of faith which heals the sick. Next we have this thought, "and the Lord shall raise him up." There could be no clearer statement of the Law of Cause and Effect, the Law of Mind in action, than this. First our acceptance, then the healing of the sick through the action of Law, relieving us of any obligation or responsibility other than that of acceptance and belief.

The Law operates upon acceptance through our belief, at the level of our faith, according to our recognition. ". . . as thou hast believed, so be it done unto thee." This is the magic key to the storehouse of abundance. Our acceptance must be spontaneous as well as conscious. That is, the whole mind must accept, the whole being must respond. We must accept inwardly, outwardly, and completely.

Conscious Union with God

". . . that they may be one, even as we are one." Jesus was praying that he might awaken the consciousness of his followers to a sense of their Divine union. The Oneness of all life is the pivotal point around which all spiritual meditation should revolve. "I am the vine, ye are the branches."

This "I Am" which is within us, is God, the living Spirit Almighty, branching out through us into self-expression. The Tree of Life flourishes in our experience when watered at it roots with the quiet contemplation of the union of the soul with its Source. Our consciousness is rooted in this Divine Presence, and should branch out into all our actions. Our actions are the fruit of this Tree of Life.

40

We are One with all the Power there is, all the Presence there is, and with the perfect Law of Liberty. We have always been unconsciously unified with good, but now that which was unconscious must become conscious. We must recognize this union and loose its power into action. Realizing that we are thinking the thoughts of God, we must know that nothing opposes the Truth which utters Itself through us.

Truth is One—"that they may be one, even as we are one." Truth is never divided against Itself. It is always available. If we would pray and prosper, we must so live that all our thoughts and acts are constructive, helpful and life-giving. Thus the Eternal Goodness Itself, flowing from the foundation of Its own indivisible Oneness, passes through us into creation.

Dominion Over Evil

Whatever apparent evil besets us can be neutralized through conscious communion with the indwelling Spirit. This is done by resolutely turning from thinking about evil, to the contemplation of its opposite, which is good. All evil becomes suppositional; good alone is real.

One of the ancient scriptures tells us that whatever is of evil is of ourselves, but whatever is of good is of God. No matter what the negative experience appears to be, the real truth about it is its exact opposite. If apparant evil says that

41

we are sick, then the Truth declares that we are perfect; if the apparent evil says that we are unhappy, then the Truth declares that joy belongs to us; if the apparent evil says that we are alone and friendless, then the Truth declares that we are never alone. We are always one with the great Reality in which is included everything that is.

Evil is not overcome by fighting it, or by recognizing it, but by non-resistance to it; by looking through the evil into the good. Thus evil becomes transmuted. Spiritual communion dissolves evil, as light dissipates the darkness. "For he shall give his angels charge over thee, to keep thee in all thy ways. They shall bear thee up in their hands, lest thou dash thy foot against a stone." Angels represent the higher activities of Mind; spiritual communion with the Infinite; the transcendent power of light penetrating every apparent obstruction, breaking down not only the walls of unbelief but the experiences which these walls have encompassed.

Not Much Speaking but Deep Feeling

"Not everyone that saith unto me Lord, Lord . . . but he that doeth the will of my Father which is in heaven." "Our Father which art in heaven" is the Divine Presence incarnated in us. The will of this Divine Presence is peace, joy,

42

goodness, truth and beauty. **We know that this is the will of God because it is the Nature of God.**

It is not because of much speaking that we are heard, but rather because of deep, earnest and prayerful acceptance. In this divine communion we should not try to think out beforehand what words we are going to use. Instead of listening to what we are saying, we should say what we are listening to; there is a vast difference between these two mental attitudes. Our words should be the outcome of a deep inner conviction which goes beyond words, but which, at the same time, gives birth to them.

There might be few words used in a certain prayer or meditation, but the words would be very meaningful. When we address the Divine Presence within and around us, we should not do so with empty phrases but with thoughts filled with the deepest sense of Reality. When we use the words "all power" there should be a reaction in our consciousness that All Power is actually loosed through these words. Thoughts, words, spoken in silence with this deep conviction, have more power than volumes merely repeated.

Anticipation and Realization

How can we anticipate unless we realize? How can we realize unless we recognize? And how can we recognize unless we believe? Spiritual com-

43

munion anticipates the answer to its prayer, recognizes the presence of the answer and rejoices in a complete acceptance that the request is granted. It sees the invisible take shape and form.

Spiritual communion enters into the joy of recognition, of acceptance, and anticipates that the Divine Abundance will provide a more lavish supply than we have ever conceived or dreamed of. Spiritual communion places its bowl of acceptance under the ever-outpouring horn of plenty, and it places its bowl right side up, rather than upside down. The Spirit can only give us what we take; and since the taking is an act of consciousness, we must be actively aware of the presence of our desire. We must know that the gift is made even before we see it. Consciousness must receive the gift.

Recognition, Unity and Command

When Jesus stood before the tomb of Lazarus, he first said, "Father, I thank thee that thou hast heard me." He recognized that the Divine would hear. He foreknew and accepted that what he was going to do would be received and acted upon. He recognized a principle of Creativity at work for him, in him, through him and around him; and in the direction which he indicated.

The next step in his prayer was, "And I knew that thou hearest me always." This was a recognition of complete unity and oneness. No doubts,

44

no fears, no uncertanties, no lacks, limitations or restrictions; no forlorn hope, no idle daydreaming, no wistful wishing. He said, "I knew." How brief but how satisfying. How simple but how absolute. There is no subtlety nor subterfuge. No denial. "I know that thou hearest me always." This is neither a wail of dispair nor a form of hope. It is free from both these illusions. It is complete unification.

Now a strange thing takes place in this remarkable prayer, this communication with the Infinite, that raised the dead and caused Lazarus to come out of his tomb. Jesus turned and in a loud voice cried, "Lazarus, come forth!" And he that was bound came forth. This is not a petition of supplication. It is not a sacrifice. It is a command. "Lazarus, come forth!" "Loose him, and let him go." Jesus spoke as one having authority. He had complied with the Law. He had recognized It; he had become unified with It; he had acknowledged the Divine Presence and infused Its Essence in his own soul. It breathed through his spirit and now It flowed forth through his word as a command—"Lazarus, come forth!" This is dominion.

The Contemplation of Reality

Prayer touches the very well-springs of our being, and through faith projects the invisible into the visible— ". . . things which are seen were

45

not made of things which do appear." This means that what we see comes out of what we don't see.

We should contemplate the presence of this Divine Kingdon to which Jesus referred when he said, "The Kingdom of God is at hand." and when he said, "Seek ye first the kingdom" because all other things are included within it.

The prayer for wholeness is a contemplation of Wholeness. The prayer for beauty enters into the Essence of Beauty from which flows the beautiful. The soul is wed to the Source of its being. At the center of our thought God goes forth into creation. This creative act is eternal, tireless and without effort.

As we contemplate the Essence of Being, our oneness with all life, that which we dwell upon springs into our experience, projected from an invisible Source which is self-energizing and self-sustaining. To contemplate the nature of Reality is to embody the Essence of Spirit with all Its power, all Its beauty and all Its harmony. The highest prayer and the most powerful, is this type of communion through contemplation.

* * *

The Prayer of Love and Friendship

"That they may be one, even as we are one. I perceive the Spirit of Wholeness, the Union of all Life. Deep within my being I know that I am One

46

with all people, all ages, all events. I am One with the Infinite and the Eternal. I am One with all the Goodness there is; One with all Power and One with the only Presence; the Presence of God in me. In everyone I meet, I perceive this union. I meet It with joy; I am accepted by It even as I accept It. I cannot reject myself nor can I be rejected by myself. There is only One Self, which is God the Eternal Self. I am One with this Self; one with Love; one with Joy; one with Friendship.

This Oneness peoples my world with the loving attention of innumerable friends, with every human manifestation of the Divine Reality. I appreciate this Friend of mine Whom I meet in innumerable forms. Everywhere I go I shall meet Him, everywhere I look I shall see Him. I am held in the embrace of the Eternal Presence. Every thought of disunion, separation or unhappiness is forever gone from my mind. Love, Joy and Companionship are permanently established in my experience."

* * *

The Prayer of the Perfect Heart

"I am a center of Divine Perfection within me. I am free from every sense of burden, strain or tension. My pulsation is in harmony with the Infinite Rhythm of the universe. There is no burden, no strain. I am not troubled nor concerned

47

over the future, nor worried over the past, nor afraid of the present. Perfect Love casts out all fear. The rhythm of my action is in perfect relaxation; its vitality is complete. The walls of my being are whole.

Joyfully the Spirit circulates through me reaching every atom of my being with the message of perfect life and happiness. All tension, fear, strain, is removed. I rest in calm assurance that Eternal Goodness is forever around me. I am free from all condemnation, judgment or bondage. My whole life is joy, fulfillment, the happiness of expression and complete freedom. There is One Heart, that is the heart of pure Spirit, that is my heart, that is at the center of my being. I sing the song of the perfect heart."

* * *

Prayer of Circulation, Assimilation and Elimination

This prayer is a recognition of the Divine Indwelling Spirit: "The Spirit within me is circulating through every atom of my being; flowing in joy; carrying the life giving Essence of Love and Wisdom, Truth and Beauty; surging through every atom of my being with Divine Power, Energy and Perfection. Infinite Spirit of Wholeness and Happiness within me—joyful is Its flow; complete is Its surge; perfect is Its circulation. Every idea that enters my consciousness; everything that

48

enters my physical being, is assimilated in the flow of this Divine Life; harmonized through Its unity and directed by Its intelligence. Every thing is assimilated and digested.

"Therefore the activity and thought of my being are balanced and perfect; every function and organ is in harmony with the rhythmic flow of the universe. Nothing remains in me but the Truth. Truth eliminates everything unlike Itself. There is nothing unlike Truth. There is no stagnation, no inaction and no wrong action. There is One Actor, acting in and through me; One Wholeness manifest in every part of my being. I rejoice in this circulation and flow of Spirit. The peace and calm of eternal well-being (the joyful recognition of my union with good; the glad opening up of the gates of my whole being that I may become saturated with the Essence of Perfection) is now complete."

* * *

Prayer for a Successful Business

Let us assume that our business has become sluggish or inactive. We then turn to the all-prevading Presence for Its inspiration and guidance in the same manner that we prayed for a physical healing, knowing that our success in business, the activity which we generate through the operation of the Law, depends upon our ability to conceive. We therefore eliminate from our

49

thinking thoughts of failure, limitation or poverty, and we pray after this fashion:

"No matter what others may say, think or do, I know that I am a success now. I radiate joy and am filled with faith, hope and expectancy. I refuse to think of failure or to doubt my own power because I am depending on the Principle of Life Itself for all that I shall ever need.

"I know that there comes to my attention everything that I need in order to project my business in every direction with the certainty of success. I see this expansion and pray that it may bless everyone who contacts it; that I may serve all who come near me; that all who know me shall feel my love and friendship and shall sense a warmth and color within me. I pray that everyone that touches my business in any way shall be uplifted and satisfied. I bless and praise everyone who is in any way connected with my business. I draw them to me with the irresistible charm of Divine Union. I serve them and am served by them. The reciprocal action of Love prospers those I serve as well as me. I am success, happiness and fulfillment."

Group Prayer

"The One Supreme Spirit is within, around and through every member of this group. Each is a center of God-conscious Life, Truth and Action.

50

"Infinite Intelligence governs, sustains and animates every member of this body. Good alone goes from them and good alone returns to them. Infinite Mind establishes harmony and right adjustment of all personal, family, business and social affairs or conditions in the life of each member. Each is supplied with every good thing. Each is happy, radiant and complete. The Spirit of God manifests in each one as Peace, Harmony and Wholeness.

"Everything that any one of this group does, says or thinks is governed by Infinite Intelligence and inspired by Divine Wisdom. Each is guided by Divine Intelligence into right action. Each is surrounded by friendship, love and beauty.

"Each person is the manifestation of the Divine Spirit which never tires, which is birthless, deathless and limitless. Each is receptive to the inexhaustible energy of the Universe and to Divine Guidance. Each person in this group is conscious of complete happiness, abundant health and increasing prosperity. Each is aware of his partnership with the Infinite. Each knows that everything he does shall prosper. Each is conscious of inner peace and poise. Each immediately becomes conscious of a more abundant life."